HE MEANT WELL

A mini guide to bullet-proof frames of mind that will change you and your relationships forever

Philosophy,

Psychology,

The art and power of language.

A guide dedicated to all those who love looking for new, better ways of seeing the world, just like I do.

Dobroslaw Karczewski, 2020

Introduction

You are truly a lucky person. The book that you are holding in your hands contains powerful knowledge. Knowledge which is not easy to find. The kind of knowledge that can change your life for better, permanently. How can this be?

It is so because it will teach you how powerful language is. In fact, language is so powerful that it literally affects everything about and around you.

Language is magic. Yes, real magic, just like when a wizard casts a spell in a fantasy world – but possibly even more powerful. Language structures your consciousness. Language can bound or unbound thoughts and possibilities.

First, let's define what I mean by 'language'. When I say *language*, I do not mean English, French, Chinese, Spanish or any other language, although your native language itself – its intonation, stress, vocabulary, order of words, grammar, pronunciation, capabilities and limitations - definitely affects who you are, and it does so on a larger scale that you could ever believe possible.

By 'language' I mean whatever you talk yourself into believing is true. In this book I will even use the word language as a verb – that you can *language* yourself into something.

But what into, exactly, can you language yourself into?

The world of possibilities is infinite. We don't really act on the world; we act on the model of the world, or *language*, that we have in our head.

Ninety percent of success in anything is creating the right mindset, the right *language*.

Perception is projection – you can design your state of mind and model reality with words. Later in this book I will show you many examples of what you can language yourself into, and some of them will surprise you.

Just think about it for a while. Have you ever considered that you can become a president of your country just by using the right words in the right order, first in your head and then outside?

No, you are thinking to yourself. That is not true. How can this be, after all? You need to have experience, certain social proof, you need to be this and that.

And I totally agree that it is not just by *saying* something – it is what saying something tells about you.

It is what saying something tells about who you are and who you have become inside.

It is how good words, at a good time and place, can help you present yourself in a particular way, make friends, make people look at you in a certain way and believe you, get inspired by you, and so on.

Just with words you can get to a place where you can run for president and win, because words are manifestation of what you think inside, and people will understand who you really are on conscious, subconscious, and totally unconscious levels.

Thoughts become words, and words become actions. The more wisdom you demonstrate the more rewarded you are by society with leadership opportunity.

People believe those who speak in a convincing way more than those who do not, because they relate good speaking with good action. "And the word was made flesh" - I am sure that you have heard that quote. Old truths are always true, we just use different words to describe the same things.

Thinking, speaking and doing – they are all linked together. First you have an idea, then you put this idea into words, and then they become action. For example, think about someone who is biased towards a certain group of people. Because they think this way, they are going to say certain words, and then act in accordance with what they believe is true – one inevitably leads to another. Then, whatever happens after that will only validate what they believed in the first place.

If a woman thinks all men are bad, she is going to manifest that with certain words and actions that will, with high probability, put men off of her. And the same goes for men who think that all women are bad. Think about one example of your own, and you will understand how powerful, or dangerous, all of this is.

We, humans, live in the world of words. Words make sentences, and sentences make beliefs and actions that follow. Those create your destiny.

Even on their own, words hold certain power and meaning (think about those bad words that you would not use in front of your dad, teacher or boss). Everyone would agree that even single words have power, and can *make it or break it* in so many life situations.

So, if even single words have power, then how much power do entire sentences have? And think how powerful whole ideologies can be? Tremendously powerful.

We all know from history that people are ready to kill millions for what they believe, and what they believe is nothing more that some words put together in sentences. Yes - what people are ready to die for are sentences made of words, put together in a certain way.

Amazing, if you think about it. You can frame everything into anything you want.

What is a *frame*?

You need to learn a term that you will see a lot in this book, which is...

Part 1

A Frame of Mind – your curse or your blessing

This is one of the most important chapters of your life.

A *frame* can be defined in many ways, so let us use a little visualization for help.

Imagine a painting. Imagine that this painting has a very ugly, maybe even a broken frame. Does this frame change the painting inside? Not really, but does it make it better in any way? Definitely not, it makes it uglier, possibly cheaper or unprofessional. Now, let's put a really, really beautiful frame around the same painting, maybe even one made of pure gold. Again, the painting itself does not change, but wouldn't this frame make it look much more sublime and majestic? Expensive-looking? Beautiful and possibly even worthy of putting it somewhere on display for people to admire?

Definitely yes. And that is exactly what frames do to us.

That is exactly what frames of mind do to you and your world.

They are a game changer. You will soon understand why.

Whatever happens, the world is what it is. We, people, are what we are. However, we can describe our reality, or *frame* it, in numerous ways.

You can choose a frame that suits your goals and makes you the kind of person you want to be, or one that will destroy you and everything around you, slowly or quickly.

Which one would you choose? The first one? That's good. So many people choose the second one. So many people choose to curse themselves, instead of blessing themselves.

I love finding interesting frames of mind. I am sort of a connoisseur of frames. I have been this way since I was a young teenager, when I got interested in psychology and philosophy.

I am in a constant search of frames of mind that can help me see things in a new, better light. Frames that can help me understand myself and the world better and deeper. Help me see things differently, in new, enlightening ways.

They could be humorous or serious, extremely deep or shallow and frivolous. It does not matter.

The only thing that matters is that a new frame that I hear or read about instantly makes the light bulb go on in my head, and makes me realize something I would not understand before.

Makes me smarter in some way or feel better about something in any way.

Makes me happier, healthier, more insightful, more enlightened, thoughtful, considerate, creative, open-minded and so on, put any quality you want or need here.

What are some examples of interesting, powerful, funny, useful frames of mind?

Before we get into that, let us discuss something equally important first.

Curses – frames of mind to avoid at all cost

If you want to make space for something new, you have to first let go of the old, whether it is material things you possess or psychological frames you have in mind.

Hopefully you do not have too many of these, but I am sure you do have at least some – like all of us.

We all have a certain emotional and psychological baggage because of where we grew up, who are parents were, friends we had, schools we went to, things we watched on TV and so on. They have shaped you into who you are today.

At this point of your life there is a huge chance that you do not even consider that whatever ideas and patterns of behaviour you think are yours have actually been, in a way, forced onto you. And... that is natural. That is how everything works.

Now, some of these patterns of thinking and doing things that you have naturally absorbed from your environment might be great for you. Keep those close.

Unfortunately, some may not be that helpful, in fact they might be ruining you and your potential. Most of these bad frames harm you just a little bit, but they still do and you do not need them. And you definitely do not need those that hurt you in a big way.

They are like a curse cast by a witch, but at this point they are even worse than that, as you are the one cursing yourself or people around you, *every* day. Very powerful, in the worst of ways.

A curse keeps you trapped in a certain condition, identity, reality.

Curses can be and are transmitted culturally.

What are some examples of curses that people cast themselves or others with, either consciously or unconsciously?

Instead of showing very specific examples, as there could be hundreds of them, I will show you certain patterns of thinking or phrases that illustrate what I mean more generally:

- I am a (put a flaw here) person
- You are (something bad)
- It is too good to be true
- I do not deserve...
- You do not deserve...
- The world is a (put a bad thing here) place.
- People are (something bad).
- I can't...
- It is impossible...
- I will never...
- I always...
- You will always... (something bad)
- You will never...
- Nothing will ever change because...
- If I try (something), I will fail.
- You will definitely fail, so do not even try
- My mother was a (something bad), I am (something bad), and so you will be (something bad)
- My country is... (something bad)
- I/he/she/they/we/you/it has always been... (something bad)
- Women are...
- Men are...

- The (nationality) are...
- Children are...
- My children are...
- Old people are...
- I hate...
- He did (something) on purpose.
- (Someone) meant bad.
- I am such a... (something negative).
- I am a victim.
- When he said (something good), he didn't mean it.
- When she did (something good), she actually had bad intentions.

And so on.

Close your eyes right now and think about similar examples.

Some of them could be even better than the ones I listed before.

Some of them could present how harmful curses are to your psyche even better.

By telling yourself and others these things, you admit that the only thing that is real is limitation and pain.

Even with my interest in psychology, philosophy and self-growth I still catch myself thinking like this sometimes, so what about your average Joe?

How much do people torture themselves on a daily basis?

What's funny is that our brains work like google for ideas. To top that off, in some ways, they are even more powerful that all search engines combined.

What does it mean?

It means that those bad things you tell yourself every day actually become true, at least for you and your world. They become your reality, because your brain will only search for and make true the things that you think about, just like a search engine gives you results of things you type in it.

In other words, your brain will make sure that whatever you think about becomes true to you, because that is how it is designed to work. It thinks that you want these things to become true, because why would you think of them if you did not?

Your brain thinks it works *for* you every time you curse yourself.

Isn't that sad?

Isn't that a huge waste of energy, potential and time? Your brain does not see the difference between a curse or a blessing, it just does its job of showing results and directing everything towards the things you put inside.

Now think about all the bad things people tell themselves every day, for years and years. Their thoughts become their reality, as solid as material things. In fact, they are solid, as neural pathways in your brains are a real thing, and those pathways can become like superhighways, superhighways of torment and sorrow.

It is very hard to get rid of such old connections in your brain. They are a huge part of it.

What can you do then?

Do not do anything with them. You will not remove them by force, do not try to fix what is broken. They might even become stronger in the process of doing so.

Instead, take something inside you that already works really well and make it even better by starting to look for new ways of thinking. Those new ways will challenge the old ways, make you more aware of them.

What is even more important though is that as soon as you start having new patterns of thinking, the old ones will naturally start to slowly disappear by not being cultivated, just like an old trail in the forest that nobody walks on anymore becomes more and more wild with years, eventually disappearing, having plants, grass and trees grow on it.

The same processes can impose limitations or create possibilities, so it is only up to you what your outcomes are.

Whatever you do gets stronger.

Whatever you do not do gets weaker.

What you dwell on is no different to your brain than what you program it to do.

What you imagine inside is no different to your brain from what you see in the outside world.

You have learned about curses, so now it's time to talk about...

Blessings – frames of mind that can help you

In my life I have found tons of interesting frames of mind.

Frames that help me see the world in a way that makes me happier and more positive, help me achieve my goals, help me attract the kind of people, situations, relationships and opportunities that I want and need to attract.

Blessings are linguistic constructs that free you, create new choices and new identities, forever.

Let's have a look at some of them.

One of the funniest one is:

"The world is my party; I am the host that makes sure everyone has a good time"

Imagine how different would your behaviour be if, as a joke, you talked yourself into believing that this was true, how differently would you perceive the world and talk to everyone.

Never underestimate the power of the absurd to break patterns of limiting thinking, behaving and responding, and this frame seems pretty good as a good start to break many limiting patterns.

Do you like this one? Feel free to incorporate this and rest that I mention into your life. You are welcome.

Another one has to do with the fear of being rejected when you meet someone you like romantically. It goes like this:

"I never get rejected; I just discover if the person I am interested in wants the same"

Think about how freeing this frame is, and how differently you can start acting in these types of situations just by thinking like this.

Definitely powerful. This one shows how *language* can either free or freeze your actions.

The next one I love is:

"Willingness is more important than confidence"

It means that it is ok to not know what is going to happen. That you should develop a good relationship with your sense of discomfort, because by doing something new and challenging you are going to feel uncertain all the time anyway.

Accept this frame of mind and you will be instantly freer to do the things you want to do.

"I will never give up on my dreams, because surrender is an outcome much worse than defeat"

Just ask any successful person how many times they had to fail in order to finally succeed.

I have heard that in the USA, on average, it takes starting a dozen or so businesses to find one that makes you a millionaire. Interesting, isn't it?

Of course, it does not mean that you should never give up on things that definitely do not serve you well, that there are no extreme circumstances you should leave behind, but what it means is that, in most situations, success comes only because you never gave up.

This one is great:

> *"I never take people's responses to me as written in stone"*

People's responses are only reflections of what they are thinking, feeling and believing at that moment.

Someone's response is subject to change and everything people offer me is just information.

Think about how, in an instant, your life and your relationships can change just by incorporating this frame of mind into your belief system, just by accepting it as truth.

Think about how differently you can start acting and approaching people close to you, or someone new that you meet.

Very profound.

Beliefs can open or close awareness, they can grant you access to powerful abilities and skills.

Beliefs tend to confirm themselves; they attract the circumstances, events and people that can reconfirm the belief. They feed on themselves.

You, in a way, engineer your own luck and coincidences. For example, by remembering that:

"People can do whatever they want; I control how I respond"

Isn't it just brilliant?

Doesn't it create a state of *uninsultibility*, making you bullet-proof when it comes to interacting with others?

Being able to choose your responses and get off of your autopilot is a magical act no worse than being able to lift things up with a magic wand. I think that it is actually equally magical, and even more powerful.

There are many blessings which, like good spells, can help you interact with others in new, better ways. Some of the most important frames are...

"People are fundamentally good"

With this frame in mind, you will treat people well, even those who don't really deserve it.

You will expect people to treat you well too, and this will become true in your world, because language not only reflects your reality, but also structures it - all possibilities are waiting to manifest and only your will decides what shifts from a possibility to a reality, only what you select with your intent and your focus.

And if all possibilities are waiting to manifest, then it is not a bad idea to choose the best possibilities there are to feed your brain with, just like with this one:

> *"People want to be good, so they respect, prioritize and are loyal to those who help them become good*

They also resect, prioritize and are loyal to those who help them find their passions, understand themselves more and ignite their desires.

Just knowing the existence of this frame of mind might change you and your actions forever.

Another frame of mind is great when meeting new people:

"Something wonderful is going to happen"

Use this frame when shaking hands with new people.

When you expect wonders to happen, they happen, because you are welcoming them and enabling yourself to see them.

With this belief you start looking at new people in your life differently, and they will feel it consciously and unconsciously, because everyone wants to be special, cool and interesting.

What's more, most people think of themselves as special, cool and interesting in some way, so they will like the fact that you treat them as such, that you show them true, unforced interest, and you will get on their good side.

The next may help you find a purpose in life:

"I am designed to influence human imagination, emotions, decisions and events"

This frame makes you understand that you and your actions matter, that you can and should create the good in this world. It gives you a sense of responsibility as well.

Can you see how useful this belief is?

It is also related to the next one:

"I must help or mentor people with talent who are less advantaged then me - this will create a great future for me, and seeing another person

succeeding is the taste I enjoy the most"

I simply love this one.

You, as an adult, have a great responsibility in shaping young people's minds and helping them.

You should want to be a kind of person who thinks this way, for the benefit of others and your own as well. Not only it is good for the humanity's future to have more people like this in the world, but it can also help you create a great life, whether financially, emotionally or relationship-wise.

Just think about the guy who discovered and helped Justin Bieber. I am sure his life had improved because of it, and that is just one little example. You yourself know many more of them.

So, go and help others if you can. They will love you for that and be loyal to you in the future. Is it not great to create an army of people who love you and are loyal to you? I guess it must be.

Once you have success it is your responsibility to take care of others, teach, mentor and train them. When you light a candle in a dark room and help someone else light a candle, and another one, you do not lose anything by doing that - they all work together.

A life-changing belief.

The next frame is crucial to your self-development:

"I can change. People can and do change for the better"

Believing this will enable you and people close to you to change.

Think about a teacher who believes in his students, compared to a teacher who does not. Which class is more likely to succeed?

Think about families, communities and whole countries, but most importantly, at least for now, think about how it can free *you.*

The next one can free you as well:

> *"I can create different selves to achieve different tasks that I want"*

This frame opens up a possibility which, up until now, has been closed in your world — that you can and should be different in different situations.

I mean, if you think about it, it is actually a very normal thing, considering that you do not behave and speak in the same way with your friends, in front of your parents, children, teachers or someone famous. If this is true, and it is, then you can grow and go beyond what you think is possible for you.

Use *identity* as a tool, or choice, rather than a fixed thing.

When you think 'it's not me, I can't be this way, I cannot do this or that', you close those possibilities and, what is much more important, it is simply not true, as what you think of who you are is just things you have done. Once you start doing new things, then *you* become something new.

Right now, you are not a singer, or a car mechanic, but you can be one if you start doing it. When you say *I can't* you are not being accurate – an accurate statement would be *up until now it's been my experience that I have not been able to.*

All of this means, that *I,* or *self*, is just a construct created by your brain. The only thing that lets you know that an act you are doing is *you* or *isn't you* is what you have done so far. Saying *it's not really me, I cannot do that* is a curse. It *is* yourself, it's just new.

How about this gold nugget? It will help you with being afraid or anxious about doing something:

"I like uncertainty, I do not mind it. Less certainty means less boundary, less boundary and limit mean that more is possible"

Most people are afraid of uncertainty, but it is only uncertainty that opens up the possibility for growth. I am sure you have heard about *getting out of the comfort zone*, possibly one of the biggest catchphrases of the century.

Familiarity can be a curse, so using it to judge what can be possible is a bad idea. Just because something feels natural does not mean that is what really serves you.

Discomfort can be that start of changing a habit pattern. If you are comfortable doing something it means it is what you're used to. If it's what you are used to maybe it is not what you have chosen, it's just what you're used to. So, bless yourself with some unfamiliarity.

I bless myself with unfamiliarity. In fact, I thrive in it.

I know that real learning only happens when I absorb, immerse myself and try to comprehend things in a palace of puzzlement, confusion, and overwhelm.

The following frames can bring you good fortune:

"The world is full of abundance, so I can be generous"

It is only in the place of scarcity that people ever need to cheat others or be greedy.

I can afford to give.

I have surplus.

I am in a place of abundance.

And also:

"I am lucky"

Luck is not coincidental.

I create my luck by blessing myself with frames of mind which lead to my lucky actions, which bring about lucky events.

"God supports me; God helps me; God is on my side; God loves me"

If you do not believe in God, then replace the word *God* with any word that suits you best – the universe, the great spirit, the earth, whatever was first, our ancestors, the higher power, flying spaghetti monster.

It really does not matter so much, as they are all just words (how powerful some of them are however), it is more about a feeling of something greater than ourselves, a feeling that we all have inside. Well, most of us at least.

Just thinking, believing and knowing that God supports you, helps you, loves you, is on your side and this will not change whatever happens can make you feel great.

It feels great knowing that you are a part of something greater, not just a random, accidental particle of dust in the vast universe.

If you do not believe in something greater than you, then language yourself into it, talk yourself into it. Treat is a self-suggestion, self-hypnosis, a useful hallucination. Some of the most fundamental aspects of our reality – what time it is, how to count numbers – are all hypnosis, suggestion, useful hallucinations. Faith has been proven to be beneficial to your mental state and is designed to do a specific task. Treat this as a placebo, and placebo has been proven to work wonders.

This goes for all of the mental frames that we discuss in this book. For example, this one:

"Once I make a decision, everything in the universe helps me achieve my goal"

It is both philosophical and logical at the same time.

When you have a goal, you start thinking, feeling, saying, responding and doing things in a certain way, and that will attract the people, situations, events and outcomes that will bring you closer to your goal. It is inevitable. Whatever you hold at the deep level of consciousness tends to be exactly what the universe shoves your way.

The next frame will help you clear your past off whatever keeps you stuck in any kind of negativity:

"Nothing really bad ever happened to me in the past"

It does not matter what happened to me in the past, as I have not consciously or unconsciously attached any meaning to it.

I rid myself of all the mind games I used to play since childhood. It's those games that were preventing me from becoming who I want to become.

This one is on a *jedi master* level of force:

> *"My focus, my will and my intent are unstoppable"*

Say it out loud: *My focus, my will and my intent are unstoppable*.

Can you feel how linguistically powerful this sentence is? Say it as many times as you need to make it a permanent part of you and your belief system.

Try to say the next one, too, until it has become a permanent part of your very being:

"I have both strong will and great imagination"

I know that I need them both to succeed.

If my will is strong, I work on my imagination; if my imagination works well, I work on my will.

Then magic happens.

Repeat the next one as well:

"I ignore and walk away from the people and situations that do not serve me well"

Being able to walk away is a powerful act, and I do it whenever I need to with no regrets.

I also ignore what is not necessary or useful to me when I learn new things, hear what people say, or read something that tries to bring about hatred, chaos or fear.

In order to improve your relationships with people, you will need this insightful frame:

"The state of my mind and the focus of my intent influences everything around me whether I consciously think about it or not, even without talking"

That is why I only choose frames that do good and serve me and people around me well.

This one will help you improve your relationship with yourself, which is the most important relationship in your life, and strengthen your trust in yourself:

"I let myself hesitate when I have to, and I let myself move forward when I have to"

I know that hesitating or acting is not good or bad, it depends on what is going on.

Allowing myself to hesitate or act is a powerful thing in itself, because it makes *me* the master of my destiny, not anybody else. *I* make decisions that influence my life, not others, because *I* know myself best, and only *I* know what's best for me.

When in doubt – I am honest with myself. I know that the ultimate authority is not authority over others, it's the authority to choose feelings and responses that I have in my life. My emotions and my responses are my employees that work for me, and it is my job to tell them what to do.

I *let* myself get into a state of consciousness, or a frame of mind, where anything can be possible, where I believe that I can do anything, whenever I need it.

I let myself be whoever I need to be and do whatever I need to do in a particular situation.

I let myself not do things I do not want to do, not to be whoever I do not want to be.

By *allowing*, I become true to myself.

I also always remember that:

"I only know a limited aspect of my personality"

And I know there is still a lot to uncover about myself, let alone the whole world.

I will not let an *identity* control who I am.

The next two are pure gold when it comes to achieving your goals:

"If someone has achieved it, I can do it too. And it's going to be fun"

And it's because:

"Everything is going to work in my favor and people are going to help me – they will give, show and tell me everything I need before I even open my mouth."

Do you like them?

Can you feel this particular, delightful feeling inside of your body when you say this to yourself? Try to remember this magical feeling, and get back to it whenever you need it.

This one can help you create your destiny in a way that you want to have it created:

"What makes 'me' is simply a set of circumstances and a set of accidents that I have experienced"

So, it is up to me to create such circumstances and accidents that will get me from where I am to where I want to be.

This one is pretty funny, and has been very useful in my life:

"Everyone is an idiot in some way"

I allow myself, and others, to not know everything.

I can be a math genius and a complete idiot at, say, cars, and that's ok. Everyone is an idiot to someone else, in one way or another.

I know what kind of idiot I am, and every time I deal with someone, I try to figure out what kind of idiot they are, so that I can communicate better.

I just love this one.

Allow yourself to be an idiot and your life will instantly become easier

Allow others to be idiots, and they will feel at ease with you.

And always remember that:

"There is no 'I' or 'I am...'; there are only patterns and frames that manifest in my behavior"

Therefore, whenever I find new, better frames and patterns, the I change.

The next one is very profound:

"Nobody can make me lose my nerves"

Well, at least in most cases, when it's unnecessary and harmful to me.

And it's because of the truth that I know.

The truth is that humans do things and respond to others and the world on autopilot, like a machine, most of the time.

How can I get angry at someone who has no control over themselves?

Who has not chosen their frames themselves, but absorbed the patterns of their immediate environment?

Who simply does not know any better?

I cannot, because I *understand* it.

Also, I observe and accept my *machineness*, my autopilot, the machine that I am, and by the act of *seeing* and *accepting* it I cease to be one.

The next one is feared by you, at least a part of you that you don't know of:

> *"What I have to do is find that part of me that doesn't want to be found"*

And then do something with it that it doesn't want to have done.

If that one was not eye-opening and life-changing, then nothing will be.

Just having a word for something, or concept for something, opens up an entire universe. In this situation, understanding an idea that there's a part of me that doesn't want to be found, opens up a possibility of finding it.

Imagine a world without the word *love*. If that word, or concept, did not exist in the language, we would not know about it. Now, just think about all these words that have disappeared from all languages, and all the concepts that have vanished with them.

On the other hand, maybe...

"There is a part of me that wants to be found"

So, I need to find it, or help it be found.

Just seeing a sentence which translates what you had going in your head, but could not put into words, can be invaluable.

It's because realization brings about results. No realization, no results.

So, maybe it's about time to realize that...

"Interacting with others is necessary for my growth as a person"

It's because people can see things in me that I can't.

Imagine an elephant in the middle of your house that makes your life more difficult, that you simply do not notice anymore because it has become so normal, so obvious, so natural to you. However, anybody will see it immediately upon entering your house.

Everyone has those elephants, whether physical or psychological, that we do not see anymore. They make our lives harder, or even miserable, and we don't even know what's happening and why. Still, they are obvious to others, and that's why they can and will be of invaluable help to me.

A couple of more extraordinary frames of mind:

"I do not let evil happen to me"

And any time it tries, I put my foot down and do not let it.

"I know what motivates me"

And I accept it.

I embrace it fully.

What's more, I use it to my advantage.

I use what I know on me. I manipulate myself in an aware, enlightened way.

I hack my brain to get the results that I want.

The next tone is mind-bogglingly powerful and possibly life-changing:

"I can be a leader; I am a leader"

The world needs leaders.

People are silently begging to be led, they want to be led, they need their leader. It is my destiny to be the kind of leader that people need.

Even if you do not become a president of your country, with this thought you will start treating people and situations involving human interaction very differently. At least on a local scale, which is also important for you, your family, your friends and anyone you interact with.

This one will immediately improve your relations with people as well:

> *"I compliment people - I like it and do it whenever I feel like it"*

Complimenting others shows that you are happy, that you like yourself and are confident about who you are. That's why you're sharing your love, that is why you have no trouble making others feel great.

People who don't like and love themselves do not tend to want to make others feel good, because they do not feel good themselves - but even they need a compliment once in a while, possibly even more so than those who are happy, so I will be the one who tells them something good.

I will tell them something good even when they say something bad to me, because I know that it's only in the frame of scarcity that people are mean and dishonest. I can handle it, I have abundance, I won't lose anything by doing it. I will only gain.

"Whenever I want to achieve something, I ask myself 'how do I make sure this happens?'"

My brain will help me get there, with its infinite power to make whatever you put into it happen.

I also challenge my brain what a question *'What if...'* to induce a state of trance and give my imagination a good practice.

The next one might sound strange, but it shows and explains one of the most important and misunderstood concepts ever:

"I am a highly suggestible person"

The most capable and successful people are highly suggestible.

I want to be one of them, so I am constantly looking for new information, constantly challenging what I know with new knowledge, with new, better ways of thinking. I do not hold on to what I know, because there is always someone more knowledgeable than me.

When I encounter something new that I like, I immediately absorb it, and check whether it works or not myself. I am not easily manipulated, as manipulation appeals to gullibility. I am not gullible; I keep the good and throw away the bad.

I have control. I create my reality the way I want and like it to be. I can, do and will choose what I learn, and this will give me what I want and need. By doing so, I will either enjoy getting what I want and need, or I will enjoy the process of learning what I need, to get what I want, to get where I want to be, to become who I want to be - who I am destined to be.

I put my focus on learning to make it happen.

The next one seems easy, but it's of utmost importance to your wellbeing and your relationships:

"I feel good"

When I feel good it's so much easier to attract the situations, circumstances, and people that I want to attract.

I decide to feel good, and when something makes me feel bad, I do not hold onto it – I leave it behind. And if for some reason I can't completely leave something behind I limit its influence on me, or look for frames that can help me see it in such a light that it stops being bad and starts being good to me, so that I can feel good again.

I feel good just by reading the previous sentence, do you?

The last but not least one touches on some basics:

"I love, I like, I am interested in, I enjoy..."

I choose to focus on the things that make me feel good. This way I can feel even better, and I can find more things that I share with people, so that I can connect with more people.

The more things I like, the more people I can speak to about things I like and have more in common with more of them, so that I can make more friends.

So, I always look for new things to like.

As you can see – the possibilities of what you can *language* yourself into are limited only by your imagination, or by imagination of all the people whose words you can hear or read – which means that the possibilities are limitless, especially in this day and age.

So, do you choose to bless, or to curse yourself? Notice how short the part about the curses was, and how long the part about the blessings was – I think you already know why. It's because, having a choice, I chose to focus on blessings, because I love them, and

I want you to know all the blessings that I have found so far.

Is it easy to suddenly start blessing, and stop cursing yourself?

The amount of energy you spend to do either of them is the same, so if you are a master of destroying yourself, then you should be able to become just as capable of building yourself up as well.

Remember that what you think is only a construct of your mind, a construct that feels so real because you have invested your focus, intent and will in over and over and over again and to make it feel real, just like a magician who invests his magical energy into summoning a minion.

Your thoughts are like minions summoned by a wizard, who sends them to do the job for him. You can create beautiful angelic blessings that will tremendously help you, or demonic curses that will totally destroy you. The amount of work is exactly the same.

One more thing – a blessing gets a lot stronger when it serves the interest of more than one person. Fortunately, all the blessings I present in this book fundamentally make everything better for everyone, so we have got that covered.

And now, let's get into a beautiful life-changing frame of mind which inspired me to write this book:

Part 2

He meant well – the mind frame that will change your world forever

Meet Karen.

Karen is 40 years old. She has a husband, two children, a dog, a cat and an apartment in a suburban area of a middle-sized town. She works a corporate job, is relatively successful financially and hopes to get a promotion soon.

Karen has problems with relationships in her life.

She loves her husband, Mike, but they argue more often than necessary. It's not that she likes doing it, it's just that she feels that her husband doesn't understand her, and that he isn't trying to change it.

Karen also has some troubles connecting with her children. To her, they often misbehave on purpose, and it makes her furious. She feels really bad having shown them her emotional side and that makes her feel resentful towards herself and shameful about being a bad mother, especially that she has promised herself to be a better mother that her mom has been to her.

At work she gets along with a vast majority of people, however there are some colleagues that, in her view, have mistreated her more than once.

Take Josh, for example.

He recently told her that the way she responds to clients' complaints could be improved and started giving her advice, even though he's just twenty-eight years old and to her it's Josh who should be learning from her. That made her angry enough to start more than a few arguments with him, and she's noticed that it has somehow damaged her overall reputation in her firm, even among people that had previously looked up to her.

She feels terrible because of that, especially that getting emotional was one of the reasons she lost her previous job, and one before that too. She thought that she got over that part of herself, but it's still there, ruining her life once again. She doesn't know what to do.

She also doesn't know what to do about Michelle, her best friend who she hasn't spoken to for almost half a year and it's tearing her heart apart.

What happened six months back?

Karen had noticed that Michelle, who is thirty-eight and single, had been suspiciously nice and even kind of flirty to her husband. She accused her life-long friend of trying to steal him from her, and decided to end the friendship. Deep down inside she knows she has done wrong, but the feeling of guilt and remorse is eating away inside of her.

What can she do?

She can bless herself with a very special blessing, so special that it made me write this book. A blessing which I really want you to bless yourself with.

And this blessing is:

"He meant well"

Or *she*, or *they*, whatever suits a specific situation.

What does that even mean?

The main premise of this wonderful frame of mind is that people, in general, are good and want good. That all people want, in one way or another, to be cool, be liked, be funny, be appreciated by others, and so on.

It assumes that nobody, excluding psychopaths or other people with mental illnesses, wants to be regarded by others as bad, impolite, stupid, boring, crazy, and such. That everything that people do, although it's not always so blatant when looking at them, is to somehow make things better, whether whatever they're doing makes sense to you or not.

So, if we assume the above, the frame *he meant well* comes to work for us and does wonders, literally.

If you incorporate this frame of mind into your life, this belief or hallucination, you will never respond to people the way you used to respond. Well, maybe not never, as it will take some time to grow into you and even as a frame master you will sometimes fall into traps of curses, but it will make things at least *a lot* better immediately.

Let's get back to our friend Karen and her life.

How could the frame *he meant well* have helped her in the past and help her now?

When it comes to her husband, once the thought *he meant well* finds its way into her conscious and unconscious mind, she will instantly start responding very differently to him. Anytime he does something she doesn't like, simply reminding herself that obviously he must have meant well (what husband would want otherwise) will put her at ease. And that is a magical skill, being able to put yourself at ease.

When you relax and tell yourself that everything is fine, that whatever those demons that you have inside of your head are trying to tell you is wrong and that you believe that someone meant well, then anger has no way to grow inside of you.

If you don't let anger grow in you, then you become a person who is in control of their responses, and so in control of their destiny. Their destiny, and destiny of others and your relations with them.

No anger equals no words you don't actually want to say.

No anger means no actions that you will regret later, actions that sometimes can ruin your life in a matter of seconds.

Now you have this pure understanding that *he meant well* - everyone does things they believe are for the good, everyone has good intentions, and everyone wants to be cool, liked, funny, interesting and appreciated by others.

Pure forgiveness – *she meant well* but it didn't work out, well, it doesn't matter, because how can you be mad at good intentions?

Isn't that simply amazing?

Simply one of the greatest things you can learn in life?

Yes, it is.

With this in mind, Karen won't be angry at her husband when unnecessary, which probably is ninety-nine percent of the time.

She can't be angry, because she knows that *he meant well*, whatever it was that he did or didn't do.

You can't be angry at people for having good intentions if you're a sane person, and 99.99% of people have good intentions 99.99% of the time.

Yes, there are some who don't, just remove those from your life, or don't keep close to them if you can't remove them.

They mean well can also help her deal with her kids. Now, with that in mind, she knows that they don't mean bad – they are just kids who don't know any better. And they certainly want to be cool and all, want to be loved by their parents, so they would never do anything that would permanently ruin that.

When it comes to Josh, her colleague, he certainly meant well as well. He wants the best for their company, in his own way, and he also wants everything best for Karen, that's why he tried to help.

Yes, there is a chance he didn't say it nicely, or something else. Perhaps he has been treated this way his entire life and simply doesn't know any better because of that, but *he definitely meant well*, no doubt about it. Knowing that, Karen would have never even thought of getting angry at him, because you don't get angry at people who mean well, remember?

Regarding Michelle – she *most definitely meant well*.

She probably thinks that Mike is a great guy, and she's really happy for Karen to have found a husband like that. She admires him, Karen and their relationship, and hopes to have a similar one in the future.

By speaking to Mike, she discovers things she likes in a man. Perhaps she was overly nice, excited or whatever happened, but *she meant well* - maybe she didn't notice something she was doing. However, getting angry at her was the worst thing Karen could have done. Everyone is worse off now.

Now, with the power of knowing that *people mean well*, even if it's not clear sometimes, she can start a new, better life, where she and people close to her can be happier than ever.

Karen has not only learned to understand and forgive others, but - and that's equally as important - to understand and forgive herself, because now she knows that she also meant well every time she miscommunicated her thoughts or emotions.

The change doesn't only happen inside of Karen's mind, as her thoughts and then actions inspire others to be the same. They incorporate this frame into their lives as well, inspiring even more people around them, making everything better for everyone, forever.

Meet Chris.

Chris is a 28-years old man living in a small town. He works at a restaurant during the day and composes music on his guitar at nights, and his goal is saving up money and becoming a touring musician in the future.

Chris has heard about the *he meant well* philosophy some time ago and it has tremendously helped him when dealing with people. He's not a master of it yet, but he's getting there.

About a week ago his father sent him a message reminding him of his mother's birthday the next day. Before knowing about *he meant well* Chris would have definitely got angry, thinking that his father doesn't trust him enough to think he can remember about his mom's birthday. He would have thought that his father thinks he's dumb and would have called him out on that, possibly starting a long-lasting argument.

Now he knows that his father meant well – he just wanted to make sure that Chris remembers. Possibly his father also just wanted to speak to him and found an excuse to send him a message. There are endless possibilities why, but one thing is for certain: he meant well.

Later that week Chris went to a mall to do some shopping.

He was looking for his favourite snacks when suddenly a security guard came up to him, accusing him of putting something into his pocket. Chris almost got angry at him for this false accusation but then remembered about the *he meant well* frame and didn't let emotions take over him and do something stupid.

A year ago, he would have started shouting at the security guard and would have even wanted to speak to the manager and get him into troubles, but now he just smiled and proved him wrong by showing there was nothing stolen in his pockets. Chris told the security guy that nothing bad happened and even complimented him for trying to do his job right.

Now, every time Chris enters this shop and meets the security guy, they send each other a wink. A few days later they bumped into each other in a pub and decided to have a beer together, and it seems they can actually become friends.

A couple of days back Chris uploaded a new song that was met with harsh criticism from his local fan base in the comment section.

At first, he got kind of angry, but decided not to write anything bad to anybody and just see what they have to say.

One comment was particularly interesting. It pointed out what others also tried to say, but in a constructive way. This made Chris rethink the composition to make it even better, so much better in fact that everyone now says that this song can become a hit.

Had Chris been narrow-minded, like before, he wouldn't have a hit song now. After all, his fans definitely meant well, wanted to help him.

What's more, the guy who wrote the eye-opening comment has become a full-time member of his band. It would have never happened had Chris got angry at everyone.

Yesterday Chris invited his parents to visit him at his place.

Upon entering the house his mom criticized him for not cleaning it often enough, but

Chris didn't talk back to her – he knew that she meant well. Maybe she was worried that Chris wouldn't feel good in a dirty apartment, or that a potential girlfriend could be put off by it. Whatever was the case, his mother definitely meant well.

She possibly could have used different wording, but maybe she just isn't able to do so due to the way she had been raised, or maybe she just had a bad day, or was really worried. Anyway, not only Chris didn't get angry, he thanked his mom and asked her for some quick tips to make the house cleaner in a shorter time, and they had a chance to talk and bond.

And what about you?

Will you get angry again over trifles at your spouse, mother-in-law, uncle, friend, colleague, classmate, boss, or anyone else from your family or social circle?

I hope not.

In the end, whatever they're saying or doing - they all mean well, in one way or another. That's for certain.

What next?

The process of learning, *really* learning something and therefore changing your life, always goes like this:

1. Insight
2. Action
3. Transformation

First you need an insight, a new way of thinking, a new frame.

Then, with this in mind, you start acting differently, because thinking always manifests in behaviour.

Finally, because your new behaviour becomes permanent, you transform yourself forever.

Thinking in a new way, or establishing new frames of mind, can and will transform you, because contemplation is the key to transformation.

And now, a big secret that all the great knew about.

A doorway to contemplation is writing things down, just like I wrote this book down. So, I invite you to write down whatever you have learned from this book, as a way to transform yourself into whatever you want to transform yourself into.

I invite you to, until your last day, always write down all the interesting frames of mind that you come across in life, so that you never forget them, just like I have written the best frames down and compiled in this book.

Who knows, maybe someday you will write an even better book about interesting ways of thinking? If you ever do, then please do let me know, I will definitely be interested in reading and learning from it.

Some things can only be learned by creating them – writing a book about something, just like I have written this book, is the ultimate step you can take. Maybe you can use even better words, or *language*, to describe what I am describing here?

I really hope you can.

You have reached the end of this book.

You've learned very powerful knowledge and I hope that you find it useful. It is short enough so that you can read it again and again every now and then, whenever you feel that you need to work on your frames. I definitely will.